Su

I Can See Angels

For my two precious angels,
Rhianna and Kendrah,
who playfully awakened me,
now I can see.

. . . .

Can See Angels

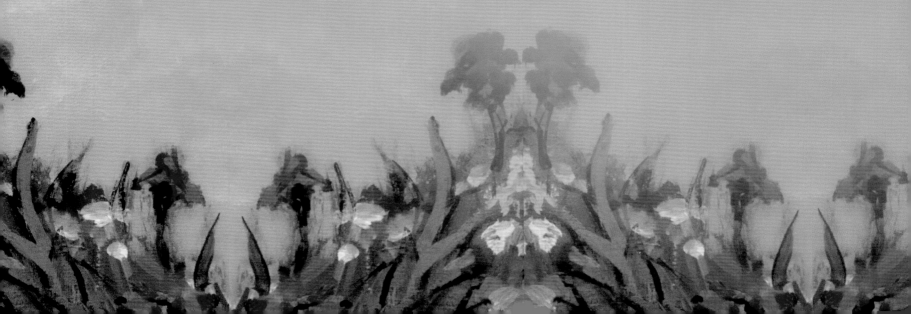

"Mummy why can't I see angels?"
Mia asked.

Above them the clouds drifted
across the morning sky.
Behind them the trees shifted.

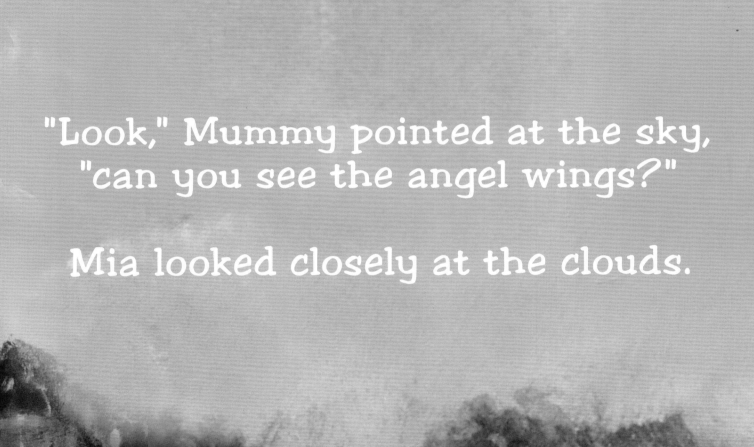

"Look," Mummy pointed at the sky,
"can you see the angel wings?"

Mia looked closely at the clouds.

One,

two,

three . . .

Mia and Mummy counted
all of the angels they could see.

Mummy held out a flower.
"Can you smell the angels here?"

Mia closed her eyes. She breathed in the sweet perfume of the flower

and imagined......

"Angels are everywhere," said Mummy.

"Even here?" Mia asked.

The flowers stretched out their floral heads.

"Yes, especially here," said Mummy.

At the park Mia flew higher and
higher on the swing.

Stretching out her angel wings she sang,

"Flying high and flying low
this is how the angels go."

From the branch of a
tree Mia swung her angel feet.
She imagined swooping down from
the clouds. Back and forth she
swooped and swung.

"Where else can you see angels?"
Mummy asked.

Mia gazed up past the top of the tallest tree

and wondered......

"Look!" Mia pointed.
"Is this from an angel's wing?"

"I believe it is," said Mummy.

Mia searched the sky for more feathers.

"Mummy," she gasped,
"there are angels everywhere!"

That night Mia held her feather
and looked out at the sparkling stars.

Outside her bedroom window the
night sky sparkled back.

"Do you think that is where the angels sleep?
Mia asked.

"Yes," said Mummy.
"There is an angel asleep on every star."

Across the sky Mia imagined hundreds

angels resting on soft golden star beds.

"Mummy," Mia yawned,